Just Beneath the Surface

Awakening, Uncovering, Discovering, & Remembering Your True Self

~ Kass Hillard ~

Other works by Kass Hillard:

BOOKS:

~ *Games Psychics Play: A Guidebook to Enhance Your Intuitive and Psychic Gifts*

~ *Journal of Intuitive and Psychic Discovery*

~ *The Final Breath: True Stories of Mediumship, the Afterlife - Messages from Heaven* (contributing author)

AUDIOBOOKS:

~ *Nevertheless, She Persisted* (contributing author)

COMING SOON:

~ *Games Psychics Play: A Guidebook to Enhance Your Intuitive and Psychic Gifts* – Audiobook

www.houseofthespirit.org
kasshillard1@gmail.com

Acknowledgments:

Thank you to Stacy Carlin for holding my hand.

A special acknowledgment and thank you to Kali of *Your Magic Words* for editing and once again making sense of my thoughts.

Cover by RLSlather/Self-Publishing Bookcovers

*****

Content of *Just Beneath the Surface* is intended for entertainment and self-discovery purposes only and not intended as psychoanalysis, psychological counseling, or behavior therapy. Seek professional help and assistance if necessary.

*****

ISBN#978-1-7347296-2-7
Library of Congress Catalog #2023900030

Just Beneath the Surface is dedicated to everyone searching for a deeper understanding of themselves. May you find the true beauty of your soul.

Enjoy the discovery!

A special dedication to my dear friend, Christina, a warrior queen, who has taught me the true meaning of perseverance.

Just Beneath the Surface

Awakening, Uncovering, Discovering, & Remembering Your True Self

"It's YOUR job to see you. It's not your family's job to see you. It's not the world's job to see you. They will see you when YOU see you."

-   **Dr. Michelle Barr, creator of the Sacred Success Coaching Program**

Parents and caregivers, clergy and teachers pour into us their beliefs about life, the world, and about God. Other family members, friends, media outlets, etc. soon enter our life, adding even more influences. We trust, believe, and accept what we see and hear as truth, rarely questioning those "facts and statements" or the source of them.

As we journey through life, we find that our thoughts and perspectives change. The more we learn or are exposed to ideas and experiences beyond ourselves, the more our world expands. We begin to question, to seek answers, to challenge our beliefs, and to find our own truths.

The purpose of this book is to assist you in discovering what a beautiful soul you are.

Each challenge offers questions or prompts inviting you to look within yourself. In doing so you will be reminded of or guided into perhaps a greater awareness and understanding of your true self, which is a spirit of pure love.

How to use this book:

Keep a journal to record and process your thoughts and feelings. It could be interesting to look back and reflect on your progress from time to time.

Allow yourself enough time between each challenge to truly reap its benefits. No more than one challenge weekly or biweekly is suggested.

After a challenge is completed, look to see if you can go even deeper with your discoveries. You may find you can. However, don't get carried away with overanalyzing. Doing so can keep you stuck.

You may choose to do the challenges in the order they are presented, or you may choose the weekly challenge randomly. Do challenge #1 first regardless.

These challenges are meant to be revealing and inspiring, but there may be some that bring up difficult feelings. Look at yourself through eyes of compassion. If at any time you find yourself needing help, reach out to a trusted friend or family member, or seek professional assistance. You will find a list of helpful resources available at the back of the book.

"Your biggest journey is the one you make within" – Janet
Nohavec

The Challenges

ONE

We often go through life unaware of why we make the choices we do.

As simple as it may seem, your first challenge is to choose a journal or notebook. It may be as plain and functional as a 3-ring binder filled with loose notebook paper, or an intricate and ornately bound journal.

Is your journal aesthetically pleasing to you, or did you not give much thought to your choice?

Perhaps you've chosen a leather-bound journal which could represent tradition or having thick skin or toughness. Maybe your journal is basic and utilitarian.

Is the color or design of your journal bold and flashy or soft and muted? Does the color of your journal hold any significance for you?

What aspects, if any, of your journal reflect your personality?

Write about your findings.

TWO

How do you define inspiration?

What inspires you and where do you find it?

Who inspires you and how?

Are you able to find inspiration in even the darkest of times?

How do you inspire others?

THREE

Every day is ripe with opportunity. Take time at the end of each day to reflect on the most important lesson the day offered you.

Did you label this lesson as negative or positive and why? If negative, what role did you play in the situation? How can you change this lesson or your role into a positive?

What did the lesson help you learn or discover about yourself?

At the end of the week look back over what you've written. Do you see any patterns emerging? Are there any areas in your life you need to adjust?

FOUR

We often think there is nothing special about ourselves, believing our talents and capabilities are commonplace and are achievable by everyone. The truth is they aren't. Even if all people could do all the same things, they wouldn't be able to express themselves in the same way as you.

What are some of the qualities that make you unique? Can you wiggle your ears? Have you got a photographic memory? Do you make the best lasagna or baked Alaska in the entire world? Are you a good listener? Have you completed a 10K or run a marathon?

If you have trouble thinking of anything "special," ask a close friend to help remind you of the talents and qualities exclusive to you.

Honor, appreciate, and respect your individualized gifts and abilities. You are unlike any other.

FIVE

Babe Ruth once said, *"never let the fear of striking out get in your way."*

It's normal and human to experience fear. Fear of change, failure, success, the unknown, etc. Fear is often the shadow of a memory of something that happened to you in the past popping up trying to keep you safe, not realizing it is no longer needed.

When you allow fear to loom large before you, it blocks your view and prevents you from seeing true possibilities and opportunities lying ahead. Fear stifles your potential, so while you may experience it, don't let it distract you from your true purpose-to express YOU fully and completely!

Ask yourself: what am I fearful of and why? What's the worst-case scenario? How likely is this to occur?

"Feel the fear and do it anyway," no matter what that fear is!

What could happen if you were fearless?

SIX

Choose a word of intention, a way of being that you'd like to focus your attention on this week. Examples could be loving, joyful, focused, or patient-whatever you would like to place your attention on becoming or having more of. Resist the urge to use a wordy inspirational phrase or quote.

Write your word on a piece of tape and affix it to your coffee cup or water bottle so you'll see it every time you sip your beverage. Put your word on a piece of paper, sticky note, or index card and place it on your bathroom mirror, car steering wheel, bedroom door, or computer screen-anywhere you will see it at least once a day. Doing so will serve to remind you of the characteristic you want to convey.

Choose your focus word wisely! For instance, if you desire to have more patience, you will be given ample opportunities to practice having patience or being patient.

"If you pray for potatoes, you'd better grab a hoe." – George Josuns

*You may find you want to turn this challenge into a weekly habit.

SEVEN

Between the internet and social media, television, radio, magazines, and newspapers, it seems we are constantly bombarded with messages that point to our being 'less than.' Our weight, hair, looks, body shape, intelligence, age, etc. are under sharp scrutiny by others, and sadly, we are often our own worst critics.

Most of us have at least one thing about our physical selves we consider to be undesirable or unattractive. For example, you may feel your arms are too flabby/skinny or long/short. Consider this: your arms can be wrapped around a loved one, providing them with a hug, comfort, and support.

Affirmations can be a great way to change your inner dialogue and turn negative thoughts into positive ones. For instance, perhaps you don't care for the shape or size of your eyes. Use affirmations to reframe your perceptions. You could say instead, *"my eyes see beauty all around me"* or *"my eyes reflect the love in my heart."*

Choose one thing about yourself that you are less than pleased with. What is that aspect of yourself capable of doing? Create affirmations to shift your thoughts. Tell that one characteristic of yourself how spectacular it is.

Start feeling love and appreciation for all aspects of yourself. You are, after all, a beautiful eternal spirit that has manifested into an amazing physical body.

EIGHT

Life often doesn't go the way you planned or expected. One moment you're traveling down the road minding your own business and then WHAM, out of nowhere you hit a pothole that rattles your bones, or you encounter a roadblock causing everything to come to a halt.

Life's roads usually display small signs hinting at what lies ahead but often neglects to have the detours clearly marked. Or perhaps you ignored the signs and signals.

When you reflect on the challenging times that appeared in your life, how did you handle them? Did you "go with the flow" or did they derail you?

Write about a time(s) life threw you a curve and something serendipitous resulted from it.

What lessons have you learned because of these experiences?

NINE

We live in a world full of abundance, which offers more than enough for everyone. Someone else's success doesn't mean there's less available for you. As they say, neither abundance nor success are pie. There's plenty to go around.

Take delight in someone else's accomplishments and achievements. Look for opportunities to offer genuine praise and congratulations. Be especially sure to do so for those individuals who seem to 'rub you the wrong way.'

Should feelings such as jealousy or envy appear, acknowledge them. Examine them. Is there a place where you feel scarcity in your life? What is at the root of these emotions? What steps do you need to take to heal your wound?

TEN

None of us started off knowing how to walk. We had to scoot, crawl, stand up, take a few steps, falter, and often fall. We received bumps and bruises and failed in our attempts many times but persevered until we mastered the skill of walking. Yet years later, we still sometimes stumble or trip and fall.

Athletes Serena Williams, Tom Brady, and Michael Jordan did not become the G.O.A.T. (Greatest Of All Time) in their fields overnight. Many of us are afraid to begin a new thing because we might not be good at it. You must become vulnerable and put yourself outside of your comfort zone to gain traction. The fact is you won't ever get better at something unless you start, falter, and gain experience.

What do you want to do or be better at? What's holding you back? How can you chart your progress? What support do you need to move forward?

ELEVEN

Elizabeth Barret Browning wrote, *"How do I love thee? Let me count the ways."*

Are you loving? Compassionate? Energetic? Persistent? Quick-tempered? No matter what, you are a fascinating, interesting, multi-faceted, and complex spiritual being living in a physical body.

Your challenge is to name at least 10 things you are.

Learn to embrace all that you are. If there are attributes you are less than satisfied with, change them. Don't let anyone else make that decision for you.

TWELVE

It is in our nature to be joyful, creative, and seek pleasure. Just observe young children who exemplify those qualities! Even so we all have moments when we feel grumpy, bored, restless, or out-of-sorts, and sometimes for no apparent reason. It's okay.

Look to see what the source of the irritation or discomfort may be. Are you doing too much or not enough? Maybe you need time to yourself or need to be around others. Are you not listening to or following the calling or longing of your heart's desire? Ask what this feeling is about and what its message is for you.

Make a list of activities you enjoy doing such as:

> taking walks or hiking
> playing with your pet
> painting, reading, or writing
> laughing with a friend
> watching movies/listening to music
> visiting museums

Having such a list handy can be helpful when you feel there's nothing to do or you find yourself "stuck in the muck" so to speak. Ask yourself what the alternative is.

"Instead of being (<u>name the emotion</u>), I *COULD* do or be (<u>fill in the blank</u>) instead.

THIRTEEN

How do you show up for others? Are you a great partner? Are you the one everyone depends on?

How do you show up for yourself?

This week, spend time alone with yourself. Do your best to silence the voices, both inner and outer, reminding you of all that needs doing, and connect with your higher self instead.

Should negative words or fearful thoughts enter your mind, be aware they are not from your higher self. Your true essence is loving and wants only the best for you.

What messages do you hear?

What guidance can you receive?

FOURTEEN

Recluses and introverts aren't the only people who want to put distance between themselves and others. Look at the ways you hide.

Do you hide behind your body size or weight?

Does your educational status keep you apart from others?

Must you be the center of attention, or do you try to disappear into the background?

What about extremes in emotions? Are you a bully or a people pleaser?

Perhaps you numb yourself with food, alcohol/drugs, gambling, work, or sex.

Do family, health, or financial issues become your reason to disengage?

Do you use circumstances or family members to become your reason for why you can't or won't do something?

When you use these and similar tactics, you prevent others (and perhaps even yourself) from seeing the real you. Look at the different ways and reasons you may find yourself not fully engaging in your life, even though your reasons and excuses may seem valid and logical to you.

How might you participate more fully in your life?

FIFTEEN

Procrastination can be a destroyer of lives and dreams. Sometimes we wait too long, and opportunities pass us by.

The Universe and everything in it are made up of energy, and you and the Universe are co-creators. This makes you capable of manifesting whatever you desire into your life. Once you proclaim to the Universe what you desire, it will act to respond in the affirmative.

Just wishing and hoping for something will not make it so. It requires desire, a plan, and action. You must do your part by taking action to receive what you desire, and being open to receiving it, even in unexpected ways. When you act, you signal to the Universe that you are serious.

What have you wanted to do that you've been putting off? Ask yourself why. As valid as those reasons may seem to you, recognize they are often just excuses or a story you tell yourself.

Start making plans to take that trip, get that education write that book, etc. ow. Don't delay. Tomorrow is not guaranteed.

SIXTEEN

All children dream of being something when they grow up, whether it be a mommy or daddy, artist, teacher, veterinarian, or firefighter.

What were your childhood aspirations?

Have you fulfilled your dreams or some aspect of them in your life? If not, what happened to make you let go of those dreams?

Do those desires still lie somewhere within you?

What are your dreams now? How can you move forward toward realizing those dreams?

SEVENTEEN

Think about and focus on your connections with others: family, friends, colleagues.

What is it about those relationships are you proud of?

Are there areas lacking? What can you do to strengthen those relationships?

Extend your thoughts to your community...state...country...to the entire planet. Is there a way to further those connections?

EIGHTEEN

Along with the list created in exercise #5, add at least 10 additional activities that make you happy and bring you joy.

Your list can be made up of things you already enjoy but be sure to include activities you don't typically do every day.

For instance, maybe you look forward to starting your day with a cup of coffee or tea before the rest of the household is up or going to the local bar with friends to have a beer and watch a game. Perhaps you find nothing better than sleeping in or going on day or weekend trips by yourself or with a partner.

Include in your list a mixture of both spur of the moment activities and others that require more planning.

Be sure this list doesn't become a "to-do" chore or bucket list.

Try doing one of these activities each day. Add to this list as other ideas arise.

NINETEEN

Make a list of the first 5 people who come to your mind/heart, whether you like them or not. Don't filter or overthink this, just allow the names to float into your mind/heart.

Jot a quick line or two to everyone on your list about something you like, love, or appreciate about them, or a special memory involving them. Consider sharing what you've written with them. If the individual is deceased, read your note out loud to them and then shred, burn, or bury it.

If an individual you listed is someone you don't care for, look for a quality about them that you can appreciate/like.

What did this exercise reveal to you?

TWENTY

They say the eyes are the window to the soul. Each day for the next week, take time to gaze into the mirror and truly see yourself, focusing on your eyes. While doing so, say these words or something similar: "I am a beautiful soul and am more than worthy." Continue looking deeply into your eyes and repeat the words.

Pay attention to the sensations in your body, to any emotions that might arise, and to your mind's chatter. Be gentle and loving with yourself.

How did this exercise make you feel? Were you uncomfortable? Did you feel silly? What do you think those feelings were about?

For a bonus challenge, repeat this exercise every time you go past a mirror for the next two weeks. At the end of that time, check in with yourself. How do you feel now versus when you first began?

TWENTY-ONE

It's inevitable—there will be times when someone says or does something that hurts your feelings or irritates you, whether intentionally or not. When this happens, instead of reacting or automatically taking it to heart, take a moment to breathe in a couple of deep breaths and send that individual a peaceful thought. Notice how doing this can transmute your initial reaction of hurt or anger into one of compassion or at least take you to a place where you have presence of peace.

You may find it necessary to establish boundaries, not only for yourself but for others. You do not need to accept poor behavior or disrespect from anyone. This is especially true and more difficult to do with family and friends. Ask yourself this question: If a stranger came to your door and treated you the way _____ does, would you allow that behavior to continue?

If someone repeatedly causes anxiety or stress, what boundaries do you need to establish for yourself?

TWENTY-TWO

Every day this week and several times throughout the day, make it your intention to be present. Focus on whatever you are doing at any given moment, instead of what will happen hours from now or what may have occurred earlier in the day. You may discover you can only stay focused for a brief period at first, and that's fine. Don't put undue pressure on yourself.

Try to be present and focused when you're doing everyday tasks such as bathing, cooking, or doing the dishes. Whatever you're doing, just focus on the task at hand. For instance, don't listen to a podcast while you're washing the dishes. Instead, focus on the feel of the water on your skin, or the scent of the dish soap. Notice the shining, translucent bubbles, hear the dishes clinking against one another as you wash them, etc. If you notice your awareness has traveled someplace else, gently bring your focus back.

Be fully present in conversations. Listen and give the other person your complete awareness. Don't be formulating your response while they're still expressing themselves. It's okay to listen, pause to gather your thoughts, and then respond.

Be here, be now, be fully present.

TWENTY-THREE

Being of service is to "be of use" or "give service or respect; to answer the needs of another."

This challenge is intended simply to answer the question: How can I serve? How can I serve my family, friends, my neighbors and co-workers, or my community?

You can choose to provide a one-time service such as dropping off a meal for someone recovering from surgery or a longer-term commitment such as mentoring a student in math. Small gestures of kindness and service go a very long way. Do all of them with a loving heart. Not everyone is destined for greatness on a global scale, but by using our talents and abilities, we can all be great in some way.

Here are a few additional suggestions:

~ knit scarves, caps, or mittens for the homeless
~ volunteer to be a guest reader at an elementary school
~ lead an activity at the local senior center
~ walk dogs or play with cats at the animal shelter
~ pick up trash at the beach or park while on your walk
~ serve on a committee or board at your house of worship or
   local government

You may never know the impact your service will have on others, but rest assured, someone's life will be better because of your contributions.

TWENTY-FOUR

What does peace mean to you? Is it the absence of conflict or chaos? Is peace when things go your way and life seems to be smooth sailing? What happens to that peace when storm clouds appear? What about tension or disputes arising?

Is peace an internal way of being? or does it come from external influences?

When adversity strikes, what helps bring you back to a peaceful calm? Can you remain peaceful in chaotic times? How do you do that?

True peace begins within.

TWENTY-FIVE

Make a list of 5 people you respect or admire, either living or deceased. What are 3-5 things you appreciate about each of them? Tally up these attributes. What qualities that show up more than others? For example, you might acknowledge 'honesty' as admirable traits for 2 of them, 'humor' for 3, etc.

Did you know the qualities you recognize in others are the same ones you embody? They are the very same attributes others recognize in you, whether positive or negative. You cannot recognize something you don't possess in some way. The attribute may need further development, but it's still there.

Consider this as well: sometimes qualities we admire in others, we admonish in ourselves, and instead seek out heavily in the people we surround ourselves with. For example, the individual who thinks they aren't creative yet loves hanging out in art galleries.

Do you see the attributes you've identified reflected in yourself? How does this make you feel?

TWENTY-SIX

Each of us makes a difference in this world to someone, whether we realize it or not. Sometimes the difference is manifested in big ways, sometimes in small ones, and these differences can vary from day to day. While you may never know all the ways, make no mistake about it—YOU matter.

This week, think of all the ways you matter and write them in your journal. Know, understand, and believe that you DO matter…every day. If you have difficulty believing it, ask others about yourself.

TWENTY-SEVEN

Whether we want to admit it or not, we all desire connection and belonging--to be part of something.

To whom or what are you connected and how? Is that relationship satisfying? Is it a healthy connection or are you enmeshed in other people's drama?

When have you felt a deep belonging? If you've never felt it, what do you feel would create that sense of belonging for you? How has the desire to belong been fulfilled?

In what way(s) can you deepen your existing connections?

TWENTY-EIGHT

Learning and trying something new keeps your mind alert, expands your horizons, staves off boredom, and can give you a sense of accomplishment or purpose.

Find a workshop, seminar, or lecture to attend either in person or online. You needn't spend a lot of money. Libraries, community centers, and colleges are great resources. YouTube is also a good option. Take an art class or join a book club. Ask someone to teach you a new skill such as how to change your car's oil or how to crochet. Maybe YOU could teach a class.

You might feel awkward or out of place in the beginning or you might feel energized or challenged. Do it either way! While you may tend to not want to interact with others, you can gain so much more by being part of a group.

Pay attention not only to what you learn educationally and what skills you gain, but what you learn about yourself emotionally, mentally, physically, and spiritually from the experience.

What ways can you incorporate learning into your daily life?

What did you learn or discover about yourself this week?

If you're feeling resistance to this challenge, you might look and ask yourself why.

TWENTY-NINE

There are times when we say or do things that bring pain or discomfort to others. It's usually unintentional, but sometimes we do so purposefully. When was the last time you needed to apologize? If it was done purposefully, why did you feel the need to hurt that individual?

Make a list of people you need to apologize to and/or actions you need to apologize for. Put aside your pride. Take responsibility for your actions. When possible, apologize directly unless doing so would cause additional harm. Make your amends and then let it go.

Refrain from using "if" or "but" in your apology, as they negate your effort. For example: "I'm sorry if I hurt your feelings but…" Do you see how these words allow you to shirk responsibility for your actions, also making it easy to give yourself an excuse for your actions and behaviors instead of accountability.

You can't control whether the other individual will accept your apology and forgive you. It's their choice. You CAN, however, control the release of any guilt or shame you may carry because of your actions.

THIRTY

Are there things about yourself you find frustrating or irritating? Maybe you become easily distracted and bored with activities which makes completing projects and tasks difficult. Perhaps it's BECAUSE you see them as projects and tasks rather than experiences.

Think of ways you can reframe or adjust those frustrations about yourself. For instance, stubbornness can also be seen as determination or tenacity. Being easily distracted and having difficulty completing projects could be interpreted as having an unquenchable curiosity or enjoying many diverse interests.

If you can't think of ways to reframe, perhaps you can engage the help of someone you trust to get ideas.

THIRTY-ONE

You are with yourself 24/7 and the chatter in your head doesn't stop. It's constant. Listen to what the words in your head are saying about you. Are those words loving, encouraging, compassionate, and kind? or are they derogatory, critical, and mean? Are they a combination of both?

Would you say these same words to someone you really cared about? If not, why would you say them to and about yourself?

This week, add more loving, encouraging, compassionate, and kind words to your self-talk. Notice the difference it makes in your attitude about yourself, your life, and others in your world.

THIRTY-TWO

The story of your life reflects the legacy you will leave when you no longer exist in the physical world, and it's being created now. We often associate legacy with family or grand gestures such as huge financial donations to organizations. Whether you realize it or not, you also leave an impact when you move on from school, a workplace, or a community.

What is the legacy would you like to leave? What do you want to be remembered for? Are you taking the necessary steps to leave that legacy?

This week, take time to write your own obituary. Try not to list only facts such as when you were born, who you married, or where you worked, but talk about who you were as a human being. What attributes do you feel you embody? What would you like to be said about you after you are no longer here?

THIRTY-THREE

Think about the loved ones in your life: your spouse/partner, children, parents, siblings, best friend, pet. What do you love about them? Why are they so special to you? How have they enhanced your life or helped to make you a better person? Tell them about it either in conversation, with a written note, or in another way that's meaningful to you. How did you feel?

What was the reaction of the recipient? Did the recipient's reaction meet your expectations? Did you have any expectations at all?

THIRTY-FOUR

Think about the one person (alive or deceased) you cherish and love above all others. Imagine you could have a few hours alone with them to share with them what they mean or have meant to you. What would you do? What would you say to them? How would they know what they mean to you?

When we become familiar with others, we can sometimes take them for granted. This week, think of ways you can make the people in your life feel appreciated. While you're at it, imagine what would happen if you treated yourself as if YOU were your most beloved.

THIRTY-FIVE

We all like compliments and acknowledgement of our meaningful contributions. Unfortunately, many of us have been taught that to feel proud of and then to speak of our accomplishments or contributions is bragging and we shouldn't do it!

Write a letter of praise to yourself. If you have a hard time beginning, think about all the good things you've done for others. Talk about the difficulties you've overcome and what was required of you to do so.

THIRTY-SIX

The Random Acts of Kindness Foundation was established by Will Glennon in 1995 in Denver, Colorado. Acts of kindness make everyone involved feel good.

This week do something kind for someone every day. Do it anonymously, if possible. Your random acts needn't be complicated or extravagant. They could be as simple as letting someone go ahead of you in the grocery line or buying a few extra grocery items and donating them to a shelter or organization in your community. Take flowers from your garden to a nursing home and give them to someone who never gets them.

Whatever you do, do something that will lift another's spirit as well as yours.

Note how you felt after each random act.

THIRTY-SEVEN

There can be times when we feel we haven't achieved or accomplished as much as we'd like or that we aren't as far ahead in life as we should be. We don't seem to live up to the expectations (often unrealistic ones) either we or society have set up for ourselves.

It can be easy to fall into the trap of what we *should* have or *should* do. We *should* have a college education and high paying career. We *should* have a spouse or partner, and family. We *should* have a fancy car, the latest fashions, etc. By comparing ourselves to someone else and how their circumstances appear to us, we begin *shoulding* on ourselves, which can make us feel unsuccessful at life.

Did you win a ribbon in 2nd grade for running the fastest? Were you a member of a team who got 3rd place in a tournament? Did you have a letter to the editor published? Did you raise a family? Did you grow beautiful tomatoes in your garden? Were you nominated for employee of the month? Make a list and write about your achievements. Let yourself recall the feelings you had about these accomplishments.

Life is meant to be a journey, not a destination.

THIRTY-EIGHT

When we feel we've been slighted or wronged, it's sometimes difficult to forgive. This can be especially true if it was done by a family member or person close to you.

Betrayal can cause us to question everything. It's important to recognize the act of betrayal is a flaw in the other person's character. Just because someone couldn't love or care about you in all the ways you needed to be loved or cared for does not mean you are unlovable.

Is there someone or a situation you need to forgive? Are you truly ready to let go? Once you do, there is no room for the story you tell about it or them to come back and take up space in your mind, heart, or life. Holding on only hurts you. The ache in your heart or chip on your shoulder are too costly to keep and too great a burden to bear. Holding on to resentment does nothing but weigh your spirit down.

Forgiving doesn't mean forgetting. It means that person or their actions will no longer have power over you. Find a way to let go of the past, perhaps with the help of a therapist. If you are unwilling to let go, ask yourself what the emotional payoff is— what are you getting by holding on.

THIRTY-NINE

Facing our own mortality isn't something most of us want to do. There are, however, some very important practical earthly matters to attend to, which will ensure your loved ones are taken care of during the most difficult and painful time they will encounter.

Make a list of important documents with account numbers and contact information. Make sure your loved ones know how to access this information.

Be sure the beneficiary on all of your accounts is up to date.

Create a will.

Discuss your final wishes with your loved ones.

How did getting your affairs in order make you feel?

FORTY

If you've ever seen the movie, Groundhog Day, you know that the main character finds himself caught in a time loop, repeating the events of February 2 over and over until he recognizes what he must do to right a wrong that has occurred.

Do you find yourself repeatedly in the same type of relationship or situation? Do you always seem to attract the same type of people into your life? Does drama seem to consistently happen around you?

If you take a closer look, you may find a pattern emerging. What is the common thread throughout? Perhaps you become too emmeshed into other people's lives and situations. This makes it easy to not look at your own issues and deal with them accordingly. You may notice the common denominator in these situations is YOU. What do you need to do to break free of these patterns?

FORTY-ONE

The people who raised us were imperfect, as were those who raised them. Sometimes we blame our upbringing or past traumas for reasons we do, don't do, or can't do something.

We like to repeat our stories over and over, not only to ourselves, but to others. In telling our story, we may find ourselves participating in character assassinations, making everyone else but us the villain. This makes it easy to forget those we blame are human with flaws and shortcomings, just as we are. Sometimes, we even place blame on situations and others who are completely innocent.

Holding others hostage to their past and their mistakes is unfair, as is being held hostage to OUR past and our mistakes. Blaming can keep us stuck in emotions and cause us to act out in unhealthy ways.

While you may have experienced tragedies in your life, it is possible to heal and move beyond them.

What stories are you clinging to?

Where do you blame others? Who are you blaming and is their participation in your story real or imagined by you?

Are there boundaries you need to establish for yourself to help you feel safe?

How do you blame aspects of yourself?

FORTY-TWO

Most of us have had periods of time growing up when we felt awkward, unsure, insecure, or lost. For some, a specific event could have been the catalyst. Sometimes these feelings became wounds and still cling to us even as adults.

Think back to the first time you ever felt these feelings of awkwardness, insecurity, etc. How old were you and what were the circumstances?

Knowing what you know now what would you tell this past version of yourself?

FORTY-THREE

Your body was designed to serve you, to carry your soul around, and to allow you to experience all the delights this world has to offer. The body you have is the only one you will get, and it is dependent on you to care for it.

Food is necessary for life. You must fuel your body properly so that it performs at its optimal level.

Do you find your joints ache after you eat bread, or you get heartburn when you've consumed dairy? Begin noticing what foods make your body feel sluggish and what foods energize you. Pay attention to what your body is trying to tell you. Give it the relief it deserves.

Consider integrating just one raw or plant-based meal into your weekly meal planning. Perhaps you can try to avoid refined sugar or fried foods or add more vegetables to your daily intake. If necessary, you may find it helpful to seek out a nutritionist or to find a food plan that's right for you.

Do not confuse what your brain says you want with what your body says it needs. This applies not just to nutrition. Is it time to give up nicotine or alcohol?

What is your body telling you?

FORTY-FOUR

It has been said people come into your life for a reason, a season, or a lifetime. Letting go of familiarity can be difficult and painful.

Has a job, friendship or relationship met its expiration date? Is it time to reassess and re-evaluate? or to gently let go and move forward?

If it's time to release, how does it feel?

Give yourself time to grieve. Allow yourself to celebrate your growth because of having had that job, friendship, or relationship.

FORTY-FIVE

Every day you wake up is a blessing. Each day is overflowing and brimming with opportunities and choices for you to make, large or small. You can build up or tear down not only others, but yourself. You can choose kindness or cruelty. You can be grateful for what you have or feel resentful for what you feel you lack. How you use the opportunities bestowed upon you is your choice.

What choices are you making?

How do you express gratitude for the blessings you receive?

This challenge is a good practice to do daily, even beyond this week. You may wish to keep a gratitude journal, writing at least one thing you are grateful for each day, with no repeats. Since you aren't repeating an entry, you may find that once you put your family and close friends on the list, it becomes more difficult to find gratitude until it miraculously becomes second nature to be in a state of gratitude.

FORTY-SIX

We all make judgements. It's part of being human. Judgement, however, is subjective and leads to labels of good or bad, positive or negative. Observation on the other hand is objective and involves the act of observing or noticing without applying a label to what is seen.

This week's challenge is simply this: love the people in your life (including yourself!) just for being who they are. Should you find yourself judging them, try observing the judgement. What does it tell you about yourself?

FORTY-SEVEN

Your body is highly intelligent and will tell you what it needs and wants. Listen to your body. Pay attention to its signals.

Perhaps you find yourself stiff and aching. The body is designed for movement. Are you not active enough or are you overexerting yourself? Exercise helps you with physical strength, keeps you limber, and releases hormones into your system.

Your community most likely offers fitness classes to accommodate your needs. There are many YouTube videos ranging from yoga and tai chi to more intense exercise. A personal trainer may also be a good option for you.

How does your body communicate with you? Learn your body's unique language and how it shares its wisdom with you.

FORTY-EIGHT

Have you ever had times when things didn't seem to go your way? It seems as if everyone and everything is plotting against you.

This week there will be NO COMPLAINING! No complaining that your hair isn't cooperating, the traffic was horrible, your children misbehaved, or this week's challenge is too hard or too easy!

Notice when you are about to complain. What physical signs manifest?

Complaining can easily slip into criticizing. Think before you speak. Look for ways to reframe your thoughts.

FORTY-NINE

We cannot move through this life untouched by pain. This week look at where you are wounded and still in need of healing.

Does your stomach drop whenever someone says, *"can we talk?*

Does the thought of confrontation make you uncomfortable?

Maybe you feel your efforts are never good enough.

When was the first time you remember having any of those feelings? Have they hindered your life in any way?

Find someone who can assist you in moving through this injury and into healing.

FIFTY

Great wisdom and guidance can come from nature. Where in nature do you feel most comfortable?

Take time this week to visit a place in nature. If it's not physically possible for you to go there, imagine yourself there. While there, listen to what the landscape and the inhabitants have to say to you.

Perhaps you have a situation or question you'd like clarity on. Ask for guidance from nature. Be open to whatever messages you receive.

What elements of nature are you drawn to and how can you bring more of it into your environment? Pictures can be a great way. If you'd like more water, add a fountain or aquarium. If the desert calls to you, cultivate a cactus garden.

FIFTY-ONE

We can experience conflict in relationship with others, with our environment, or even ourselves.

This week, rather than being concerned with being correct or right, or needing to have the last word, ask yourself what role you play or have played in the conflict.

If you had a disagreement with someone, were you trying to force your opinion or will on them? Were you trying to get your way without listening to the other party's wishes, desires, or opinions? Was your tone in the exchange curt or dismissive? Truly listen to what the other individual is saying and attempt to understand their point of view. This doesn't mean you need to agree with each other. You can still have mutual respect. Can you find a commonality?

Look into the mirror and see what attitude you're wearing today. Does that attitude look good on you? Perhaps reach deeper into the closet for a different attitude to wear. Maybe you need to add some understanding to go along with that sharp or rigid opinion.

FIFTY-TWO

Are you the one everyone leans and depends on? Let someone else be strong for you this week.

Try asking for help or assistance. How did it feel? Was it difficult and challenging for you or did you find it easy and a bit of a relief?

FIFTY-THREE

This week make a conscious effort to wear something that makes you feel special. It could be an item of clothing, a piece of jewelry, a special cologne, or a new hairstyle.

Notice how this small change makes a difference in your energy. Did you find you had more confidence? Did you feel sexy or sassy?

Did it change your interaction with others? Consider what it would be like to feel this way most of the time.

FIFTY-FOUR

Your body is your temple, and it requires regular maintenance. This week you are being asked to take care of your physical body.

Are there health care issues you've been neglecting to take care of?

When was the last time you had a physical or dental exam? Is there a patch on your skin you need to have looked at? Is your diabetes or high blood pressure going untreated?

Is there therapy or counseling you need to pursue? Do you have an addiction you need help in controlling? Make appointments if necessary.

FIFTY-FIVE

Write a love letter to your body, telling it all the wonderful things you appreciate about it. Start at your head and go all the way down to your toes. Don't just focus on what you see externally. Your brain, internal organs, body fluids, etc. all deserve praise as well.

Is there a part of you crying out for attention and to be noticed? a part that has been neglected and desiring to become whole? What is it saying to you? What does it need from you? How can you heal that part of you?

FIFTY-SIX

A mission statement is the *"formal summary of the aims and values of a company, organization, or individual."*

A personal mission statement can help define who you are. It can remind you of your purpose and help you to stay focused during chaotic or difficult times.

Think of yourself as the CEO (Chief Executive Officer) and board of directors of the corporation of YOU. How do *you* wish YOU to be represented? Ask yourself what ideals you wish to emanate, to be a representation of you. Remember that these are ideals, not goals. They are principles and virtues to strive for.

Where to begin? Make a list of attributes you feel you embody or ones you wish to. For example:

   compassion honesty intelligence strength peaceful humor

Choose a few attributes and develop an affirmation or mantra that you feel best reflects your core values, one that you can use daily. It shouldn't be longer than two or three sentences. For instance:

- I am a compassionate human being
- I seek truth in every situation
- I am grateful for all I receive
- I listen thoughtfully and move through my world peacefully
- I find peace in every situation

(continued on next page)

For extra fun, create a mission statement with your partner or family. What does your partnership or family stand for?

Here are a few prompts to get you started:

- We love and care about one another. We show it by…
- We support each other by…
- In our household we….

FIFTY-SEVEN

Altars are shrines of dedication, created to honor, remember, or inspire. They can be any size and can be joyful, playful, serene, or inspiring. All are a visual reminder of your connection to Source, to ancestors, and to your heart's desires.

Create a special, sacred altar space in your home or garden using items with special meaning to you. Consider creating one in your workplace as well.

FIFTY-EIGHT

"Truth is One: Sages call it by various names" – Rig Veda, 3000 BCE

How do you define spirituality? Do you see spirituality different than religion? In what way?

What was your perception of God/Spirit/Creator when you were a child? How did you learn this?

Is this perception still true for you? If not, how has it changed?

What conflicts has your perception of God/Spirit/Creator brought to your life?

How important is the role of spirituality or God/Spirit in your life?

Do you believe in a power beyond yourself? How do you define that power? Where or when do you most feel the presence of that power?

Do other people's spiritual beliefs threaten or challenge you? In what way?

*****

I hope you've enjoyed these challenges and that they've brought you a better understanding of yourself.

You are a powerful spiritual being cloaked in an amazing physical body. Embrace your gifts and share them with the world.

In Peace,

Kass

IMPORTANT NUMBERS

National Suicide Prevention Lifeline   988

National Alliance on Mental Illness (NAMI)   1.800.950.6264

National Domestic Violence Helpline   1.800.700.7233
or text START to 88788

National Sexual Assault Hotline   1.800.656.4673

Substance Abuse & Mental Health   1.800.662.4357
 Service Administration (SAMHSA)

National Council on Problem Gambling   1.800.522.4700

NOTES

Made in the USA
Monee, IL
04 March 2023